Wakefield Press

SWEET RIVER

Jack Hibberd has written over sixty plays, including *A Stretch of the Imagination, Dimboola, A Toast to Melba, The Les Darcy Show, Captain Midnight VC, One of Nature's Gentlemen, Three Old Friends, The Overcoat* and *Peggy Sue*.

He has published three novels: *Memoirs of an Old Bastard* (1989), *The Life of Riley* (1990) and *Perdita* (1992), and three volumes of poetry: *Le Vin des Amants* (1977), *The Genius of Human Imperfection* (1998) and *Madrigals for a Misanthrope*.

Jack Hibberd graduated from Melbourne University in 1964. He worked as a medical practitioner for many years and retired in 2019 from his position as a specialist allergist at a Frankston clinic. Over the years he has been a member of both the Literature Board and the Theatre Board of the Australia Council. He also held the Vice Chancellor's Fellowship at the University of Melbourne through 2019 and was the Founding Chair of the Australian Performing Group at the Pram Factory in Carlton.

His son, Spike Hibberd, is a graphic designer working in New York where he designed the cover for this book.

# *Sweet River*

poems

JACK HIBBERD

Wakefield
Press

Wakefield Press
16 Rose Street
Mile End
South Australia 5031
www.wakefieldpress.com.au

First published 2021

Cover designed by Spike Hibberd
Typeset by Michael Deves, Wakefield Press

ISBN 978 1 74305 860 2

 A catalogue record for this
NATIONAL book is available from the
LIBRARY
OF AUSTRALIA National Library of Australia

 Wakefield Press thanks
CORIOLE Coriole Vineyards for
McLAREN VALE continued support

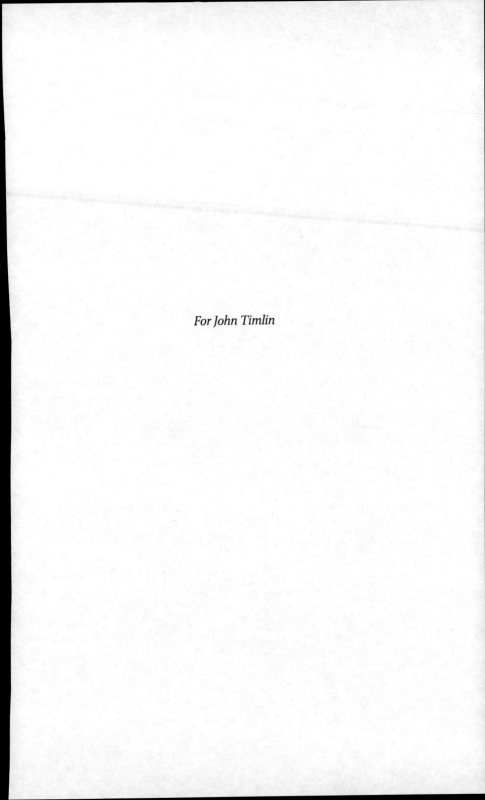

*For John Timlin*

# Contents

# INTRODUCTION

BARRY OAKLEY

To understand *Sweet River* one needs to understand its author. Putting things crudely, there are at least two Jack Hibberds: an outerman and an innerman. The first is the famous Hibberd, who back in the 1970s led the pack of radicals, Marxists, blowhards & junkies that made up the Australian Performing Group.

They offered a new kind of theatre, that scorned the proprieties of the Melbourne Theatre Company – for a popular, accessible form. Hibberd had the right words for it. 'A theatre that intermingles celebration with satire, fun with gravity, fiction with information, and slang with poetry.' In other words, make it local, make it communal, and if necessary, make it offensive.

And if you didn't mind the bare boards, terrible coffee and shabby surrounds of the Pram Factory in Melbourne's Carlton, this is what you got – and a lot of what you got was Hibberd's: *The Les Darcy Show*, *A Toast to Melba*, a vaudeville wedding spoof called *Dimboola* and *A Stretch of the Imagination*, now regarded as a classic.

But there was also an innermost Hibberd, who, when the APG were not fighting amongst themselves or the middle classes, retired to his study and wrote poetry – that was as different in its own way as his plays.

First in 1988 came *The Genius of Human Imperfection*, a collection that was epigrammatic, angry, cynical, even splenetic:

> Have a perfectly rotten day,
> Septic, may all your gold teeth fall out,
> Your hair moult including the eyebrows

May you shed your thick skin like a snake.

(Have a Nice Day)

Six years later, in the aptly titled *Madrigals for a Misanthrope*, the lines still burn with a cold fire:

> So it has come to this,
> an awareness of bone,
> cartilage and marrow
> an apprehension of skin,
> fissures, flakes, feral hair ...

(Leaf Drop)

The body fails, & love does too:

> Are these the last days of love, love,
> when not only do we grow brittle, old
> but the bed-air between our bodies clings cold?

(Disaffection)

And now, after seventeen more years of cellaring, comes *Sweet River*. But something has happened. There's no irony in this sweetness. The title poem is pure lyric. The lines are longer and seem to swirl with the water as it makes its way to the sea.

And in the wash of water and words, there's an implicit message. Humanity might be the great polluter, the river's enemy, but it will all live on, preserved in language – language that seems to lighten Hibberd's usual dismal subjects – decay and death. We get the full gloomy monty in this collection, ending with a joyless 'Ode to Joy'. But there's always the sweet river, pristine & beautiful, memorably mirrored by a master wordsmith.

Barry Oakley

## SWEET RIVER

At her source among competing alps she tentacles
and zigzags, a silver trickle in the sunlight,
between upholstered moss and whipped grass,
across laminated schist, over flattened pebbles.
Occasionally, surprised, she plummets, gurgles
in a deep green pool (where graylings, tadpoles, flit)
or bounces, sparkling, off basalt and granite.
Abandoning lichen, bracken, our stream is greeted
by ferns, reeds, riparian blooms: yellow, lilac,
plum, cerise, vanilla ... investing her royal blue.
Now broadening, and deepening, the flow
becomes less swift, but potent enough to powder
sandstone, limestone, splinter toppled trees.
Then, among alluvial plains, old willows weep,
and pollens from pasture grasses talcum her skin.
In anabranches plump trout pretend to doze,
while crays cakewalk, out for carrion.
At dawn, gorillas, peacocks, mammoths, unicorns,
approach to drink and watch kingfishers dive for fish.
By noon, serenity and silence govern: nature's siesta.

Now a giantess, no stream, no river, but an estuary
where her vast waters disembogue – unless confronted
by a moon-empowered sea's attacking tide.
Customarily, however, she transports nutrients
and maternally feeds the tiniest and lowest specimens
of an oceanic food chain, contributing to a world
that is elemental, natural, selective, scrupulous,
if vulnerable and naïve – before the descent of man.

## WATER

It either trickles
or thunders,
executes colossal rolls
or sleeps sheet-flat.
It can glisten like silver
or old gold,
be true blue
or chlorophyll green,
define translucence,
or simply quench.

In prelapsarian times
tadpoles wriggled like sperm,
rainbow trout snapped at flies,
the platypus prevailed,
and hippopotamuses laughed.
The seas and oceans
thrashed with fish,
undulated with porpoises,
were graced by albatross,
shearwater, shag, and pelican,
surprised with spouting whales
in tribal pods,
over which flying fish flew.

The Mediterranean is now mud,
the Amazon toxic to piranhas,
the anchovy extinct,
and the last whale
dead, beached on Nagasaki beach.

# DOWNPOUR

The rain slams against the mansion's weatherboard walls,
against sheets of glass and a grand gothic door.
Lightning bifurcates, electrocuting the heavens.
Thunder grumbles, reverberates, like supersonic booms.

Waterbirds flock back, waders wade, their curved beaks
(resembling scimitars) stab, pierce, and scissor
through swamplands, holding high clawless crays, flat worms, and
unfinned fish. They fight and feast and die.

The mansion broods upon a hill, towards which
speed a lioness, hyena, zebra, and a unicorn.
They are followed by two pretentious emus, one
screech owl, a lovebird, a stork, and doddering dodo.

A gorilla beats its chest on the roof, a rattlesnake
rattles around a satellite dish, some bees and butterflies
look lost. The temperature plunges: snow descends.
Two crazed rhinoceroses smash down the door.

Soon the mansion is cramped with animals. Some munch
on corpses, others snooze on beds, others again attempt
to copulate: a warthog mounts a mongoose. A dove
drops dead. Waters rise rise, but the mansion does not float.

# FLOODS

*I.M. J.G. Ballard*

After devastating droughts, floods will ensue.
At first raindrops will pop and puff up
the fine dust, giving off that distinctive smell
of mushrooms, shovelled earth, and shaken ivy.
Drizzles will thicken into ropes of water,
vertical sheets, rinsing lashing inundating all,
creating swollen tides of mud, and writhing slime,
on which no human foot will impress or squelch.
From now life shall begin again from below,
among simple and increasingly complex molecules:
algae, water weeds, amoebae, protozoa, germs,
then in an epoch or two, the indispensable worm,
of soil and sea, crawling across Sahara's ocean floor,
around the sunken ruins of London, Athens, Rome.

# LAKE

*for Will Henderson*

An elliptical shape, whose surface often glittered
blue: cobalt, cornflower, teal,
depending on the season and the sun.
Despite its amplitude and beauty, this sheet
of water, mysteriously, at first sat unpopulated.
When humankind first became erect,
then sapient, gatherers and hunters traipsed
around the district, until attracted by somersaulting
fish and massed migratory birds,
after which villages were thrown up on each shore.
Coracles and canoes were built from skins and bark,
while the women pestled buckwheat into flour,
and combined that with feeding an Ogg or Miff.
The men at first confined their wading and vessels
to the shallows, where they skewered somnolent trout.
With the invention of the paddle and rudder,
providers soon propelled themselves to the centre,
then disappeared ...

Wives and mothers wailed and sobbed.
This travesty was repeated numerous times,
until the lake district everlastingly lost its allure
to humans,

but not to fish, fowl, and crustaceans.
Eels and little worms wriggled sensuously,
dragonflies swivelled their ceramic torsos,
pelicans scootered in, and circumflexed their wings.
This became an uncivilisable paradise
for nature,
its true Arcadia, Cockaigne, Eden
and Elysium.
And so remained
a mystery ... despite technology, exploration, science, facts.

## DAYBREAK

Dawn splits her giant opalescent bell,
and first light leaks through the air.
Birds, eyes cocked, are the first to tell,
as the last fox scarpers to his lair.
A rooster struts, yodelling done. Crows
survey the chattering chicks beneath,
while kookaburras and wattlebirds throw
their voices Handel-like at the east.
A gormless work turns, and is gobbled up.
Women turn, yawn, and stretch their thighs.
Silk slides, clavicles shine, hips are cupped:
dawn's melodies are tempered by raucous cries.
Children pop out from soft dreamy sheets,
and bicker, as they brush their savage teeth.

## WISHFUL THINKING

At last here comes the rain,
may it be a downpour,
again and again.
Let the downpipes and conduits roar,
the gutters cataract,
and streets streak like rivers.
May the reservoirs once again brim
and saturate all arid plains and plots,
until wheat, rice, and barley bristle,
while vegetables sprout, and fruits plump up,
finishing famine in the slums.

May this deluge in part be acid,
sulfuric, carbolic, and selective,
singling out and favouring the Vatican,
Wall Street, Beverley Hills, Miami,
the IMF, World Bank, and the City,
honouring celebrities, fashionistas,
the Chicago School and Friedmanites,
corroding neo-cons and ecorats,
until they too are skinned alive.

Yes, this will be pennies from heaven for the poor,
and a tumbling down into the Styx for the rich.

# DROUGHT

It is not just a lack of water ...
dry cracked creek beds, dead bulrushes,
brown ivy clutching at hot stone walls,
magpies, doves, gasping in the shade
of oleanders, peppercorns, and gums,
but the lack of everything:
skies devoid of clouds, the stagnant
windless air, the silence of starlings,
no dogs at dusk in winter, nor roosters flapping
though dawn, the barn owl whose barn
has collapsed, crushing carpet snake and rat.
Unlike the dehydrated explorers of yore,
there are no vivid mad hallucinations
of hope. Instead, green eyes desiccate
and shrink to minute white peas,
visionless, while tongues, tasteless,
cleave to corrugated hard palates,
unable even to clack or slide
like a slug across cement.
This is final mummification,
not a single wriggling Baudelairian worm,
not even one of John Clare's weevils
to nibble away in a natural feast.
This is when bodies literally decompose
into dirt, granules, grit, and dust,
not within coffins, crypts and graves,
but on the surface of the earth,

barbecued by a mushrooming Copernican sun,
billions of us contributing to the sands
(not any compost, tilth and peat beneath)
of an undulating global Sahara,
finally parching Burma and Bangladesh,
whitening the Black Sea,
burying the Dead Sea, and in the end levelling by erosion all alps,
until the atoms of Democritus
deliquesce into the quanta of nothingness.

## A SMALL DROUGHT

The house squats on the hill,
and creaks, since it is early evening.
The windows, oblongs of light,
gaze out across the paddocks:
stubbled barley, wheat and oats.
A pennant of pearl smoke drifts
distractedly towards pink Venus.
A rooster mounts a hen, and crows.
Starlings swarm, swerve, twist
to bed, within a giant cypress.
The family, stuck on windowsills,
digest their gravy beef and crusts.

A grey mother soaks salted cod.
The children blow bubbles.
Father clenches his soft fists.
The water in the last tank is low.
A baby plays with his penis.
In the distance a pig shrieks.
This could be a time of severed wrists
and throats, of blasts, moisture, rest.

# HILL

They did not settle here for the view,
but desperately scuttled up from the plains,
where they had been pursued by Neanderthal
remnants, bull-browed brutes wielding massive clubs,
or grim Romans, phalanxed, with their walls of shields,
thrusting short blades, and intrepid silent tread,
or Vikings with egg-white eyes, herring breath,
helmets, broadswords, and hardened penises.
Terrified survivors dug ditches, threw up ramparts
of blocks of rocks – above needle-sharp wooden stakes.
Some centuries on the hill progressed
to masonry, slit windows, and battlements –
over which boiling pitch was poured on naked Scots.
During certain reigns Castle Hill incarcerated, tortured,
Catholics, their Jesuits, Anabaptists, and Jews.
Presently some of these heretics were axed
through the neck, and their heads paraded
through the streets and squares of a festive city.
From the eighteenth century until the 1960s
Castle Hill found itself a sanctuary for lunatics,
where the 'Gogol cure' (leeches on the nose) was favoured,
until the miracle that is electroconvulsive
therapy occurred, along with slow axings
of the frontal lobes, and sweep deep insulin comas.

Castle Hill now luxuriates in chamber music recitals,
quilt-making classes, gymnastics, chess,
a pudding club, foxtrot nights, and ping-pong.

## VOLCANO

Visible for at least thirty miles,
steam, smoke, and ash, hiss
from its massive upright nostril,
defeathering moronic birds
and caking grey the ruddy slopes.
Occasionally spouts of orange flame
lick the blackened sky, and form a fabulous fountain.

In an ancient epoch
this puce cone was both feared
and worshipped by the denizens
of those lower lucerne-green shires.
Naked virgin girls were flung
into its purgatorial orifice
to appease, propitiate,
their vengeful unpredictable gods.

Today, there are no gods ...
(and a paucity of virgins),
because all is explicable,
and every secret manifest.
Hence our volcano's sad slumber,
and the self-complacency, aloofness,
of its new obdurate city, Sisyphus,
which has hauled itself up to the heights
through laborious endeavour.

The volcano was deemed extinct by volcanologists.
So, Sisyphus soon reached its crater's lip.
Tourists lounged on balustraded balconies,
and peered down into its dead gullet,
until one pink autumnal dusk
brown magma suddenly shot up and spilled over,
deep-frying celebrities, wellness
charlatans, tycoons, and volcanologists.
The rivers of lava only ceased
their flow and flood on arriving at the Lethe.

## HELL

The sun emits a class of heat
that castigates our wantonness.
We see Shakespeare's blasted heath,
tumults of tropical insects
swarming northwards, headed for Antarctica,
to which still travel ships of fools.
In bungalows around the Equator
sheets of plate glass melt, and dribble.
Populations roast and crackle, as if on spits.
Gigantic salamanders, fire-drakes,
dance as if to Stravinsky, snort and feast,
competing over stillborn babies.
New volcanoes bulge up, celebrate
with Bables of ascending smoke
and magma's ponderous cascades.
The seas become impromptu casseroles,
brown not green, sweetly simmering along,
a recipe that unites all civilizations,
with beasts, from hyenas to dugongs
… as Manhattan tumbles down.

## DEATH WISH

The earth would flourish
without humanity.
Leave it all to the worms
and ants and bees.
The ladybird would return
and snack on aphids, thrips.
Salmon would once again hurtle
up translucent rapids.
Several buried eggs
of the long-dead once-waddling dodo
would hatch in exultation,
liberating clamorous chicks,
fed by festive cormorants and shags.
And home home on the range
only deer and buffalo would roam,
while humpbacks could hump
without fear of the flensing Japanese,
while jackasses, coots and kookaburras
would shake the new blue skies with mirth.

# IMAGINATION IMAGINE

*a flat patch*

Inspiration seldom if ever apprehends me now.
My genie sprawls, half-comatose, pure phantom,
or even worse, a smug and contemptuous ghoul.
Part of me is dead; possibly that figment gland,
due to a valetudinarian shrinkage of the heart.
Erato, Erato, whisper something into my ear,
invigorating, evocative, an echo from the past,
a rhythm, familiar footfalls, so I can again feel
... forensically. No artifice and no persiflage:
they muffle silence, a preferable emptiness.
If not, I shall give up the ghost, bleach each page,
or scoop up my oeuvre, and fling it into a furnace.
Beckett said: imagine imagination is dead.
I exclaim: imagine imagination alive instead.

## ALL AT SEA

I stand upon a dune,
eluding razor-bladed grass
and rocks: my feet are bare,
oedematous, the colour of prunes.
Land for me evokes the past:
youth, middle age, dotage,
everything for which I do not care.
So, fixed, I face out to sea,
no longer daily hostage
to bombast, business, humanity.
I feel as free as a zephyr,
and watch the skuas dive-bomb
for fish. An albatross appears
with golden seaweed in its beak.
A dozen silver dolphins stitch
the limits of the olive undulating water.

Distant voices call me back:
mother, father, children, wife,
and a few friends as well,
but all of this to me now is strife.
I do not possess the resources
to sit down, comingle, talk.
I watch the ocean's cream horses.
I butterfly out, as light as a cork,
then lie prone, speed above black wracks,
until smashed against the rocks.

# DANDENONG PSYCHIATRIC HOSPITAL

*May 2001*
*delusion*

It's grim to believe that you're sane, and be cooped
up in a lunatic asylum, with thirty fruitcakes.
Though one other chap believed himself sane: Herr Walter
Wahl. While my beloved wife had me certified,
Walter was committed by a wife and two daughters.
He was an educated bloke, from near Munich,
a roly-poly Bavarian, and only slightly medicated.
Most of the other guests behaved like zombies,
whereas Walter spoke speedily, alertly, unzapped.
After he overcame an initial diffidence
we played pool several times a day. Inevitably
Walter won: his Teutonic assiduity and precision cut
through my volatility and bumptiousness, a jackanapes
against a calm methodical introvert, who flicked
balls into pockets, rather than smashing them to death.

I wonder what ever happened to Herr Walter Wahl?
I hope he is free, like me, of that oubliette and hell.

## MEGRIMS

Frequently I am consumed by sadness,
not suicidal, nor remotely whimsical,
somehow closer to the satin French: *tristesse*.
Angst is part of this ... sepia instead of black,
resembling some moderate fever, a nimble virus,
which leaves no cell, or film of fluid, untouched.

It doesn't seem to stem from rebuff, loss,
let alone obnoxious acts, or insults that I fling.

Perhaps it is Joseph Conrad's 'national spectacle'
that I view anew ... monstrous pullulations of peoples,
and the threatening lobal inanition?
Perhaps this occurs because I am fatigued with life,
a victim of a monk's accidie, and anomie?

## IT IS TIME TO MOVE ON

And put it all behind us
(the treacheries, the blood, and guilt
- that strange itch). Let us move forward,
all smiles and public push,
our backs well-protected
by stab-proof quilts.
We now face nothing untoward,
nor threatening. The fact we've said
these things somehow conjures
up immediate expiation.
Once we swore: I stand
by my words – so help me God.
Now one insolent ejaculation,
as trite as an ampersand,
will see history abjured.

But the poet's inspiration
predicates that these sods
will amble to a precipice,
and grinning at cameras,
continue forward in space
and plummet down to fire.
Others will jog to a crevasse,
in whose depths wait dire
anarchists and sans culottes,
who never forget the past.

But art is useless ...
despite our patronage.
We will never face the music.
The Dantes of the world are pests,
despite the grisly punishments of their infernos.

Time does not now exist,
and space resembles centrifugal mucus,
the past a fraud.
This enables us to cheat,
and ensures that we are readily believed,
that everything indeed has disappeared behind us,
and below our fluorescent balconies,
the globe's exonerating chorus
applauds.

# CREATIVITY

*for Spike*

The cogs are now locked in
with gnashing flashing teeth,
an exquisitely tuned machine,
an invention in itself,
a Tingueley conglomerate aberration,
of acrobatic free wheels, long pistons
that punch the air,
of lurid thrashing feathers, foghorns,
little tunes on metallic plates,
simple harmonic emotion,
infinitely adaptable,
and absolutely useless
(in the efficacious sense),
but a source of quick astonishment,
magic, and renewal.

## MOZART

Mozart was interred within a pauper's grave,
for which there is no trace.
He discovered fame in Linz and Prague,
as well as among the Viennese,
until they coughed him up,
as if he had the plague.

He, like others, well ahead of their time
(the C Minor Piano Concerto: Beethoven's favourite),
failed to appeal to fashion's chime.

The list is long:
from Bizet to Schoenberg,
while others, favourites of the throng,
all won ecstatic accolades,
for works now dead and buried.

The mystery is this;
one genius will enchant an epoch
(Johann Sebastian Bach and Verdi),
others, no less inspired, will have to wait,
until time and enlightenment catch up.

Do we know when his unfinished Requiem
was first performed?
Did Sussmayr organise one,
beside his grave perhaps,
with an orchestra of keen Czechs from Prague,
with chorus and soloists from Salzburg.

## BRAHMS

A man who grappled with creativity,
who could fashion music like a blacksmith,
many compositions being hammered, stretched, into shape.
The strains and tensions on display
as motifs contend with themes,
as anguish tempers the threat of hot elation ...
climaxes that never quite come to orgasm.

A lonely gentleman, morose in the cave of symphonies,
he found relaxation in the drawing-roomish sextets,
but felt much more at home before his piano,
and with the violin, the voices of his unattainable loves.

# ON REREADING SAUL BELLOW

*a prosaic poem*

He makes the late John Updike seem creamy, shallow.
The latter's undulant urbane New Yorker prose style
exonerates much of an America that is on the nose.
Saul excruciates, intoxicates: less mellifluous, more wild.

His Jewish characters, schlump or mensch, blend as Yanks:
full of chutzpa, braggadocio, anguish, sex, and chicken.
Bellow's creations ride beyond psychology: the sane or cranks. These
vivid contrivances are phenomena, furiously driven.

Not merely larger than life, they exhume, extrude, a new life,
or make entire fools of themselves, amass colossal fortunes,
sell hessian in Hester Street, conduct searches of the soul, strive to
escape a family, tradition: Litvak knuckles, suffocating bosoms.

Yet in the end Bellow has most likely not hatched one great
novel – except perhaps *Herzog*. Others can uncouple, slide,
drift away. Nevertheless, the oeuvre, bit by bit, aggregates,
integrates, into a strangely hallucinogenic whole of some size.

By contrast, Updike, a waspish Ivy League mandarin patriot
and 'realist', seduces, suavely exculpates his fellow Americans
throughout the 'Rabbit' quartet with a paucity of guns, gunshots:
here he is the most egregiously Edenic of literary Republicans.

I have not reread anything of Updike. I do not have the time,
or impulse. John wished to be remembered by what he wrote.
I fear he will not endure, owing to a wallpapering design. Cheever
presaged all of Updike, on a more dangerous note.

Rereading Saul hasn't made me mourn the loss of this Chicago man
who flings at us a theatre of clouds, fierce sleet, alchemical sunshine.
Inside every outrageous or dull-dog character lounges the Bellow
man: shrewd, philosophical, erotic, witty, mad, and very very fine.

## ARTAUD

So far yet so near
are the realizations of my dreams,
when those carnivals of the bizarre,
will play to packed tents, to screams,
to tears, and all-consuming mirth,
when the sawdust turns to tinsel,
when blood gurgles up through the earth,
when audiences emulate minstrels,
sing to their children of sweet peace
and hard love, throbbing necks noosed in wreaths,
when the future re-engages with the past,
and sees the same the same, but twice as fast.

## OPTIMISM

I have no name
and live in squalor,
enfeebled by cholera,
beri-beri, rheumatoid arthritis,
and galloping pneumonia.
My eyes at dawn are glued,
but separate by noon.
It's then I set off for lunch,
through yards of Carolina slime,
to the local dump,
a festive place,
where scraps are shared
with Southern charm:
head-butt, bullet, knife.
Thus sated
I slither home,
and tunnel into bed,
a bag of bones.

One day I'll recuperate,
grow another leg.
I shall never be an ingrate.
My table will spread and spread.
Gorillas, swine, and rats will be my guests
of honour,
waited upon by human pests.

# TRANSIENCE

The theatre ship sailed forth,
after a crack and panache
of fine pink champagne
on her sabrelike bow.
Lemon-coloured streamers
stretched and then snapped.
A band chorused out jazz
in Jelly Roll refrains.
Upon the pier crowds
danced and applauded.
Silver waves smacked
her gilded hull,
while around the rear churned
deep green water from the deep.

Actors packed the decks
... all in character:
Lady Macbeth, King Lear,
Feste and other Fools,
Mephistophales, Krapp,
Woyzeck, Mother Courage,
the Lord of Misrule,
the Government-Inspector,
Goldberg, Death, Medea.
the Three Sisters, Ubu,
Don Juan, Saint Joan, Lady Bracknell,
and a sneering Alceste.

This troupe of troupers
all acted their pants off,
declaimed simultaneously,
gestured tellingly,
as they dwindled into specks,
soon not discernible.
The audience remembered to remember,
as the ship became a golden blister,
at the base of a high thickening pall.

## THE SAME

Here judgements tend to be twisted:
the spoilt brat who can do no wrong,
an admonishing teacher harangued,
the bullying son who becomes the victimized.

Families can defend to extinction
their psychopathic boys, abusive dads.
Wives, smashed in the face, husbands
bitched until bonkers, seldom complain.

It is the same regardless of breed,
bent, religion, politics, ethnicity.
The toiling classes club together,
mingling pugnacity with suspicion.

The lumpen-middle classes snootily
peer down, and slavishly peer up.
Their ordinariness is a social glue.
Complacent masks camouflage disgrace.

The English aristocracy once dispatched
their ingrates and cads to Australia.
Today's toffs hire bloodthirsty legal packs,
so their escutcheons hang unbesmirched.

Sameness fears disrepute, disintegration,
since familiarity sustains survival.
The brazen salvage of public face
seeks to shield lies, crime, and stupidity.

## THE OTHER

They look different to me:
the hooked nose and full lips,
or slit eyes and mustard skin,
the flattened square occiput.

She speaks with an accent,
or in an unfamiliar tongue,
and exceedingly loud ...
with froth around her mouth.

He gives off an uncouth smell
of ferment and putrefaction,
not exactly halitosis,
since emanating out of pores.

She wears a black tented dress
and a pink veil across her cheeks.
That expression seems supercilious,
as if I were insignificant.

These people crowd in on me:
they immigrate, they populate,
disrespectful of borders,
and my quarter-acre block.

But I am vigilant: a broadsword,
crossbow, mace, Winchester,
automatic rifles, stun guns,
and instruments of torture.

## A TREE

I once had a black wattle
which ennobled my whole garden.
Its lime-green filamentous fernlike leaves
formed traceries against the charcoal
of trunk, twigs, and branches.
Some of the last cantilevered very high,
others fanned out unusually low,
affording windbreak and shade.
And when its blooms exploded
the tree completely entertained,
as if sprinkled with party lights,
blending colours of loquat, cumquat, and quince.
Flocks of birds would swoop in to feast:
technicolour king parrots, lovebirds, rosellas,
white cockatoos, and philandering galahs,
all chattering like an orchestra before a concert,
a concert at which no conductor would arrive,
until instead their hilarious harmonies were drowned
out by the humourless cacophony of a chainsaw.

## CACTUS

I think of the cactus:
bristling with needles,
exceedingly prickled,
yet its up-curved limbs
are welcoming ...

Inside it's juicy
to the point of succulence.
That is how the thing survives.

It seems lonely,
since standing by itself
in a vast desert,
nevertheless proud
and monumental.

Frosts alternate with great heat.
Tumbleweeds tumble past.
Coyotes howl with pleasure
as they copulate.

A noble but dolorous sentinel,
the cactus blooms
but once every seven years.

# HORSE

Why does a horse look so sad,
depressed, when alone in a paddock,
enclosed by fences and a stable?
Its noble head droops down,
staring at half-nibbled grass,
or, high, peers vacantly
into a smudged distance.
Although within a spacious area
a single horse does not trot,
canter, gallop, or kick up dust.
Even a long carrot
does not dispel the animal's gloom.

A scrutiny of Franz Marc's
Expressionist rendition of horses
in a feral mood
revealed to me this:
the horse is a beast of the herd,
and is at its happiest
when in the company of others.
That is why brumbies seem to grin
as they speed across Australia's outback,
together, and free of humankind.

Otherwise, when on funerary duties,
like Pegasus, all glee, it flaps
a heroine or hero
down to Heaven,
and up to Hell.

## GALAHS

Unlike the goose
or cockatoo,
galahs are rakes
and hussies.
The glue
of nuptial
and de facto
couplings
does not adhere.
Attired in smooth
love-dove grey
and flaming pink,
these Don Giovannis
and Moll Flanders
flirt and seduce
among wattle trees
and pasture grass.
This is why
they crop in flocks:
untrusting,
because a harem
and a troupe
of sugar-laddies.

## BLACKBIRD

She or he squatted on a nature strip,
dead. A small ruby bead of blood
gleamed above an inert eye. Its tail feathers
were fanned out wide, from before, to balance.
The wings were tucked in, circumflex tight,
preserving heat ... before a rigor mortis
refrigerated all. No doubt it had been whacked
senseless: once this would've been a shanghai's
pebble, today some careering Mack truck.
So serene, so presentable, an admonishment,
blackbird essence, resembling a life study
in sculpture, on a sheet of green, all ebony,
except for a bright citrus beak,
and that ruby bead of blood.

A sad spectacle, but not as sad
as the one I had seen the previous week:
a duck lay squashed flat,
red in the middle of a black road,
and on an emerald verge opposite
stood its husband or wife,
staring, quacking, in deep staccato bursts,
from isolation and desolation.

# COCKIES

*for Molly*

Sulphur-crested cockatoos are here in teeming force,
flocks packed on power lines and cruciform poles,
flecking white the russets of autumnal ash.
They have flapped for hundreds of miles,
away from devegetated plains, grey hills,
dams and rivers emerald with algae,
in search of quenching water and nutrition:
the season's final figs, pomegranates,
quince, and cotoneaster's bitter fruit.
The segments of their crests separate
into elongated tensile sails
as they screech and screech,
much more vociferously than before ...
their stomachs shrivelled and dyspeptic.
This will be a long cold winter,
sitting huddled and fluffed up in black ironbarks.
Not a few will fall off a twig,
and land agape on asphalt or dead grass.

# BERT BRECHT

*Carlton, 1968*

I once housed a canary called Bert Brecht,
his cage secured against a kitchen wall,
opposite a window favoured by the sun,
the morning sun, a signal for Bert to whistle.

Above his cage sat emblazoned a Brecht quote:
'I never warm the cockles of a heart.'

We utilised, exploited, Bert Brecht
for my play *Who?*. His cage dangled on stage,
suspended in bleak dark. When the lights flamed
Bert thought dawn had arrived, and trilled away.
This invariably provoked applause.

After the last performance of the season
we roistered, with Bert, downstairs
backstage, until the crack of dawn.
I remember crawling along with torn flares,
and waking up the colour of a cooked prawn,
stupefied, my mouth an arid lesion.

Late next day, somewhat sallow, I thought of Bert,
and sped to the theatre, then backstage.
There he was, still in his uncovered cage,
but upon the floor: stiff, inert.

# GAEA

(i)

Suddenly the snarling winds howl,
avulsing roofs and chimney stacks,
sheet metal shoot like towels,
bricks become as light as flax.

People staggering along outside
are stripped of clothes and hair,
then the tempest flays their hides.
They crawl: knees and elbows bared.

Sad pleasure craft dock in streets,
penthouses are buffeted, smashed.
Tall office blocks shudder, creak,
oscillate comically, collapse.

Families circulate helter-skelter
inside homes plucked and shot up.
Some find traffic tunnels, war shelters;
if not, the thickening hail cuts them up.

Soon torrents supplement the typhoons.
Levelled cities are engulfed by lakes.
Next a massive tidal wave looms,
the legacy of an unearthly earthquake.

(ii)

The storm slices through the high trees,
oak, cypress, sycamore, eucalypt, ash,
while the valleys choke with leaves,
most shredded from being thrashed.

Their trunks stand tall, denuded, stark.
Long elastic twigs twist, ache, and snap.
Ripped-out branches drop past bark
and out of wounds oozes precious sap.

Soon they topple into midden-mire,
among chain-saws, corpses, garbage,
with flecks of phosphorescent fire:
all fuel for a new carboniferous age.

Cyclones pitilessly accelerate,
ululating around the universe,
as humankind self-mutilates,
and Mother Nature spits out her Widow's Curse.

## SENESCENCE

With the exaggerations of age
our works now scoot by,
equal to, when we were young,
long extended days.
The last lunch, a week back,
seems to have been completed
just twenty-four hours ago ...
as I clamber down to pluck a bottle of red
from my cobwebbed cellar.
This cruel companion of time
must presage death.
For me that haste is harsh.
I imagine for others who
endure pain, stiffness, wheeze,
dumbstruck senior moments,
who require a walking frame, a pacemaker,
and swallow twenty pills at breakfast,
this speed must appear blissful.
Death where is thy sting?
To the contrary, I leap out of bed
(after having ravished the wife),
take a cold shower – it being winter –
attack some rump steak and eggs,
compose a sonnet or ballad,
hand-mow the front lawn's buffalo,
freestyle numerous laps of a pool,
read a tranche of *The Man Without Qualities*

turn off some insipid Delius,
then finally pluck a magnum of Gigondas
from my frigid catacombed cellar,
and head off to lunch with the blokes,
who all resemble Methuselah.

## SENESCENCE AGAIN

The nights are now so long.
The days race by.
Not that there is a heap to accomplish ...
weed the garden,
sink a few bulbs,
shovel up some sods,
trim the weeping willow and its yew,
lubricate my walking frame,
take our spaniel for a promenade.

I imagine it is the light
that accelerates events,
the blazing of a distant window,
the cataracts of sunlight,
water like a silver mirror,
green memories that mass
and block until day is done.

The nights grind past ... out,
I imagine it to be the gloom
that applies some brakes to a chap,
the crashing into rubbish bins,
the starless evenings,
yes, failing vision
despite the bright haloed halogen lights,
the reading reading of books
in giant puerile print.

I wish the nights would shrivel
to a few hours long,
and my days stretch long long and long.

## RECREATION

What will become of us?
We feel like lemmings, jubilant upon a cliff.
Yet will we be rewarded with a Noah's ark?
Yes ... a pair of earthworms,
three cockroaches, one slug,
a quartet of mosquitoes,
and a pride of maggots.

With the waters rising, rising,
I'd conjecture
that the future of the human species
resides with the slug.
Besides exhibiting a zeal for moisture,
the slug is a reproductive wizard,
copulating with itself.
A penis and vagina in one.
Such ingenuity
and narcissism
should eventually
reproduce a template for the human race.

## SUPERSPECIES

It is said that we are distinguished
from animals
by our consciousness,
fire, our ability to cook,
to stitch together clothes
and strum the ukulele ...
also our knack with words,
artistic wizardry
and philosophical zeal,
our towering religious instincts:
the very acme of evolution, breed.
Yet, should we abruptly
all become extinct,
drop dead en masse,
the earth would steadily readjust:
regenerate, recreate, diversify.
For the flourishing and bloom of this globe
we have become far less essential
than the empires of ants and worms.

# GRANDIOSITIES

It's the big things that count,
a billion dollar win at a casino,
the ravishing of a Venezuelan Miss World,
the rustling of ten thousand superfine merinos,
taking my custom-built Ferrari for a hurtling burl.

It's when I lead a coup d'état in bankrupt France
and reign as King Louis the Nineteenth,
when Prince Harry weds my daughter Constance,
and that Venezuelan Venus becomes my Queen.

It's when I buy Corbusier and Lloyd Wright houses,
then level them to raise post-modern follies.
It's when night after night my man Max and I carouse
on Petrus, Mouton Rothschild, La Tache: constantly jolly.

It's when I purchase England's bullion reserves,
and have cast a giant gold statue of myself,
finally planting it on top of Marble Arch's curve,
then watch Beefeaters guzzle to my health.

It's when I snap up the whole of Tasmania
and expel (repatriate) its dimwit whites
to the dead cities of continental Australia,
when Aborigines return: new totemic rights.

It's when I lie on a death bed of ortolan
feathers ... not entirely painless, succoured
by my Bangalore mistress, and a brass band
attacks Mozart's *Don Giovanni* overture.

# MINUTIAE

It's the little things that count:
the mint sauce upon a lamb chop,
a twinkle in an eye,
a new vegetable in Bangkok,
a stranger on standby.

It's when the subtle is strong
and nuance resounds in waves,
when an Alberti bass becomes a song,
the discernment of chlorophyll in hay.

It's when the unspoken utters,
a daddy-long-legs dances a tango,
a love letter found in a gutter
the first munch on a mango.

It's when the hangman winks,
and death dissembles a delirium,
the bunch of everlastings on a coffin,
a free slug of Jamaican rum.

It's the invitation to a dance,
the beautiful woman who passes
by, glimpsed merely for an instant,
a chorus line of arses.

Yes, the little things add up:
the mathematics of existence
as applied to happiness.
Disaster can multiply by increments
(occult cancer, carbon excess),
but is more likely to exponentially erupt.

## SETBACKS

They customarily bolt from the blue:
the neck of a femur's sudden crack,
a cobber's flattening by a branch of a yew,
the unexpected stab in the back.

The brakes that vanish as you shoot
down a hill, and collect a thoroughbred.
The son who overnight becomes a galoot:
a spiced drink rendering him brain-dead.

The wife that elopes with a wealthy chump,
a bore who can empty a whole club;
a virulent attack of the mumps,
testicles shrivelling to peas-sized nubs.

Your magnum opus obliterated by fire,
abrupt incurable pestilential flatulence,
a financial advisor's and accountant's dire
embezzlement leading to prompt indigence.

Or a citizen who enjoys life on the streets,
in a chaff bag, bright blue from the cold,
magenta chilblains, frostbite of the feet,
until smacked flat by a truck, out of control.

# GOOD & FAITHFUL SERVANT

*London*

Grey days pad pad past.
The mercury slides down to zero.
My alarm clock laughs.
I catapult out of bed: a hero.

I slave away for thirteen hours,
attack my PC's keyboard
as if a virtuoso, never sour,
producing spread-sheets galore.

Though twice down-sized,
I still stroll on my stumps
to work, full of corporate pride,
since I'm constantly beneath the pump.

The days are actually quite short,
my nifty screen's a work of art.
I love bangers, mash, a glass of port,
lifting dumbbells, flinging darts.

As to my golden handshake,
the CEO gave me prostheses,
a seven hundred share stake,
and a ticket to the Andes.

# PERSONALITY

It's an elusive quality,
particularly when a person does not possess one.
Yet even among those without,
there exists diversity and nuance.
For example, a chap might enjoy the personality
of a speed hump,
while another seems a corpse that walks.
A third can be an insipidly sad robotic bank teller,
another a billionaire bamboozled that her wealth
does not purchase, invite, keen interest.
Then a cove might be so devoid of facial élan
as to adorn a niche of waxworks
dedicated to non-identities, non-entities.

Again there are those who are injured, stung,
by the impact of their protoplasmic social torpor.
They become aggressive Argus-eyed, manipulative,
transmogrify into predators, on the prowl, to prey
upon bright sparks, wits, shits, cards, and lions.
I speak of bores.
At gatherings a bore will corral his quarry
in a corner (or among cactuses), deaden all vivacity
with flat fatuous loquacious cant
and pitiful oddly mesmeric eyes.
The victim either pleads a protuberant bladder,
or slides down the wall, stupefied.

Remarkably, women are much less afflicted
with this vacuous and Parkinsonian blight.
I surmise an anthropological genetic aetiology.
A lady cannot be an able communal gatherer
of nuts, seeds, wild fruit (and a chatterbox)
unless she commands gregarious presence.
Yet a crack hunter can flaunt the personality of a log.

I would have thought, hoped,
that natural selection,
the irreproachable tastes of women
with respect to men,
might have bred out these dull dogs by now.

Where are you Charles Darwin?

## DEAR DARWIN

The last of the first human beings
seemingly was not an existentialist,
nor did he appear religious.
Because he's not much remembered now,
let us christen him Adam.

Disenchanted with civilisations
and their suicidal sophistications,
he retreated into caves
(troglodyte and speleologist),
equipped with rations, batteries,
a pedal generator, you name it.
When these supports become exhausted,
he adapted a Lamarckian fashion.
Once almost entirely without hair,
the cold soon provoked hirsutism.
A diet of slugs, black eels, and bats,
saw Adam as slippery as slime,
and with the vision of an owl.
Ballet, music, analytical philosophy,
he didn't much miss: long lost in the past.

Nevertheless, Adam did eventually miss
another: company ... companionship.
He composed epistles, reveries, and tracts.
On introital walls he ochred ... lust.
He bass-drummed the ribs of his chest,
bellowed like a cowless bull seal

(or mammoth given his prolific pelts),
and emerged to face a fierce light.

Fierce because it ricocheted off sand,
Adam's pin-point eyes gradually dilated
and revealed domains of dead plains,
without etiolated grass and lean weeds,
without lizards, vultures, scorpions,
but with cromlechs and cairns of human bones.
So dehydrated he resembled a giant
ginger hairball, Adam rolled onwards
until he saw a towering cruciform cactus.
Six-inch needles pierced his cheeks
as he gnashed its thick green carapace,
and sucked out succulent liquid.
The sands soon gave way to grass
in bright green tufts, then violaceous shrubs.
Next he relished shoots, roots and rhizomes.

Then one Wordsworthian afternoon,
Adam found himself beside a pink lagoon,
and there on an undulating green bank
lounged the last chimpanzee,
with big brown eyes and lilac breasts:
it was love at first sight.

Thus recommenced a natural selection,
and a re-evolution of the human race.

## HOLLYWOOD BOWEL

There in the front row seat the dwarfs:
Alan Ladd, Humphrey Bogart, Tom Cruise,
and the vulgar spoiled American super-brat : Shirley Temple.
Behind them sprawl hundreds of hams,
not excluding the Paragon of them all: John Wayne
with his fatuous rugged handsome features,
his inability to act,
his monotonous repetitions dead flat drawl,
which enshrines an American tragedy:
tough-guy jingoistic navel-gazing ignorance.
Beside him sits James Cagney, forever grimacing,
then Marlon Brando, smouldering with humourless gravitas,
next Victor Mature, with that oscillating Adam's Apple,
and numerous gullible graduates of the Method School,
who could all do with a long dose of the Marx Brothers.
But they are not here.
Instead we have the little tits and the big tits:
Katharine Hepburn and Princess Grace,
Jane Russell and Marilyn Monroe.
And along the back reside
the studio producers, the big bosses,
(chiefly Jewish)
who brown-nosed McCarthy, betrayed colleagues:
directors, actors, designers, composers,
some of whom had, ironically,
as Jews, fled from Europe,
and were compelled to flee again.

They sit expectantly before an empty stage,
increasingly desperate for some action:
song-and-dance, teeth and smiles, colour and movement.
Instead a quite surreal phenomenon begins to assert itself:
the audience members liquefy, coagulate, congeal,
into one extensive turd,
which concertinas and congas off and away,
until it comes to rest at last
along the length of Sunset Boulevard.

## VANITY'S HUMAN WISHES

Vanity was fair,
from a head of frothy curls
to curvilinear toes.
Her face waltzed, despite being firmly
and classically modelled:
pert nose, cushioned cheeks,
ruby Mona Lisa lips,
and avid spinach-green eyes.
It possessed a beauty
that stopped men
(and some women)
dead in their lubricious tracks …
the sight of her cream skin
compelled them to ogle and paw the air.
Vanity's neck arched
elegantly like that of a ballerina,
then plunged into sinuous collarbones
between plentiful shoulders.
Her breasts, conical but soft,
occupied the whole of her chest.
Below, in their shadow,
sat a concave abdomen
and deep repoussé navel
(made for digits and long tongues).
And below that flourished
lush lemon pubic hair,
and long nutmeg lips

and little pink lips
and a pert noselike clitoris.
Vanity's thighs nestled,
or jostled against each other
as she rearranged herself
before an obstinate and rigid beau.
Her knees,
as with all women,
resembled those of a camel.
Vanity's calves, however,
made chaps summon up mangoes.

Last, but not least,
were her ankles,
as trim and as finely turned
as those of a road-runner
– not that she ever ran.
No. Vanity's pulchritude
predicated languor, serenity,
dentary queenliness.

The tracts of time
tracked Vanity.
Her face creviced,
and neck turkeyed.
Her breasts dangled down
to a patulous navel.
Her lemon pubes greyed
around a shrivelling quim.
Those thighs blubbered,

those knees grated,
and ankles ballooned.
Bunions leathered
and tormented her contorted toes.

Vanity sat before a mirror,
employed all the oils
and unguents of the East.
She sought masseurs,
spas, reflexologists, quacks,
but to no avail.

Vanity sat before a mirror,
and sobbed and sobbed,
not because of a loss of beauty,
but that her vanity
had left her utterly alone:
no mere man had ever been good enough.

# SYCHOPHANTS

They are a piebald species.

At one extreme puffs up
the toady, who reflexly smiles
a broad ingratiating smile,
before, say, a radiant celebrity,
a power-mad politician,
or a junk-bond billionaire.
Invariably a male, this lickspittle
in the presence of, say, a Mrs Thatcher,
a First Lady, or a Mother Teresa,
releases a film of perspiration,
and can even grow concupiscent.

Then there is the fawner, wheedler,
and yes-person, out to advance
his or her lot in the world.
The victim is forensically selected:
a specimen in a position of power,
narcissistic and vain.
So, an ego is cajoled, caressed bewitched,
then the popinjay's manipulated:
positioned for the stab in the back.

At the other extreme prowls and struts
the sycophant of the Iago ilk,
another adulator ... but of evil.
Unlike the amphibious toad
or tradesmanlike tuft-hunter,
this exemplar is an artist:
he plots, he charms, he plants, he charms,
until the candidate self-destructs,
or becomes homicidal.
Here sycophancy is the other face of hate.

# MISERS

Meanness is a cast of mind,
cohesively wrought long ago,
an adamantine growth
which has squeezed out all generosity.

One class possesses super wealth,
owing to its innate stinginess.
I imagine exemplars only cackle
when ogling bank accounts,
or lifting up a bar of bullion.

Another class inherits wealth.
They are customarily bachelors
or spinsters, too parsimonious
to share a life, with either sex,
too tight-fisted to foster children,
too pennywise to lodge a pet.

Then there are the mean and poor,
who dine on cans of dog food
and parrot seed, who rank a feast
some suet on a slice of toast,
and, like Third World orphans,
rummage through bins and rubbish dumps.

In the end all these skinflints
must find rapture in misery,
and the moneybags must be egotists,
immune to loneliness,
besotted with their own sterling company,
its sad sad gold and silver linings.

## SADNESS

An endless dead-flat plain
of lime, tufted with dead grey grass,
a satrapy where it never pelts,
the sky a motionless miasma of mist.
Here there resounds the muffling of sound,
and even pungent refuse does not impinge.
All touch inspires touchiness.
Appetites crave vinegar and gruel.
Libidos lust to be left alone.
Dreams entirely disappear,
and nightmares conflate with consciousness.

Unlike Orpheus, one cannot look back
... to the towering palaces behind,
to all the colours of the rainbow,
to spinach-green hills and valleys,
reverberating with birds and bulls,
redolent of daphne and jonquil,
where undulating lovers bleat,
and orchestras articulate sweet Beethoven,
and the skies blaze a brilliant blue ...

instead of grey on white, and white on grey.

# THE DUX OF TEARS

Sometimes sorrow squeezes up, a sinister glue,
unpredicted, unprovoked, indivisible …
a feeling without feeling, numb yet true,
and eerie, silencing everything remotely risible.

Beneath all this swarms fear, foreboding:
comprehensive, unfocused, and vast …
a heaviness as heavy as a heaving ocean,
and, in a sense, catastrophe's peculiar ballast.

Soon fear cannibalizes sorrow into gloom,
the octopus of hopelessness inks my air, the sack
of the body bloats, blocks out all room,
and suicide becomes a flippant act.

## LADIES' MAN

He was the most dashing corpse I have ever glimpsed:
decked out in that grey, light blue striped Prince of Wales
check suit, mother-of pearl-blouse, plus a mango tie.
His chestnut hair undulated in sets of foppish waves.
The seasoned undertaker (who moonlighted as a face-lifter)
could not compel his customer's eyelids to clamp together.
The eyeballs defiantly protruded, coloured apple green,
and glistened. Those long thin arms, again recalcitrant,
were folded in nonchalant repose behind is oblong skull.
I could have sworn (standing there, wrinkled with stark
grief) that his nostrils dilated, then his mouth and jumbo jaw
slid, ever so subtly, as in life ... before complete seduction.
Old habits die hard. Yes, I could discern that familiar
impudent bulge, and the lineaments of a sweet leer.
Even in death Dave was nifty. I let him iron out my wrinkles.

# A PUTRID MARRIAGE

There is little worse ...
the constant venom and its cant,
each mouth expertly pursed,
yet emitting florid rants.

Their king-sized primrose bed
all but bifurcates.
They sleep toe to head,
like halitotic prison mates.

At dawn Serena scratches flesh,
Patrick, on top, jabs away ...
bleeding cheeks and bruised breasts:
a two-backed beast of prey.

Even after separation,
and a crisp decreed divorce,
there was still vituperation:
a love of hate their one genius.

## SONNET

To write a sonnet is to execute a dance,
for some. For others it's arranging masonry.
For others again much more is left to chance,
where sense meets frolicsome serendipity.
For most iambics thunder, march, or lightly trip.
For the heterodox syllables and cadences compel,
where sound is a texture of dactyls and anapests.
Contemporary poets relish more the villanelle,
for its hypnotic, elegiac, choric power ...
or the sestina, with its escape from demanding rhyme,
into free loquacity: then that taciturn envoi.
Yet the orderly sonnet disorders the mind,
so that unexpected associations delight,
as when Shakespeare wields his far-flung might.

# SILENCE

*for*
*Gerald Fitzgerald*

It can indeed be golden,
so sacred to Flaubert,
somnambulists, and cloistered monks.
It is when nature hibernates,
when owls cease to hoot ...
and Beethoven gently fades away.
It is the gulf between
every prolix sentence,
when contemplation reigns.
It occurs when reclining on a rooftop,
with ears securely muffled,
oblivious to the city's rat race,
the gibberish of apes,
and children's spoilt cacophony.
It's that escape from pandemonium
of bibulous wives, sport, and the stock exchange,
a military band's blast of brass,
the crass fatuity of talk-back,
a traffic's incessant screech,
and that of women having sex.

It is each philosopher's hermitage,
and artist's sanctuary:
Aristotle on Parnassus,
Montaigne in his tower,
Bishop Berkeley inside Stonehenge.
It's Villon's solitary confinement,
Cezanne contemplating an escarpment,
Wagner on the Matterhorn,
T.S. Eliot deep down a bank vault
... each folded in a sepulchre of silence ...
white outside, but pure gold within.

## DOWN MEMORY LANE

The scent of frangipani saturates the air.
She sports a red hibiscus in her soot-black hair.
A distant church's bells toll toll away.
A lapwing flaps and throttles through the dusk.
A moon slides up, as yellow as warm hay.
She stands close. She smells of passionfruit and musk.
Her eyes resemble embers, lit up by bellows.
Her nostrils flange. Her lips palpitate.
I shuffle. She makes me feel quite callow.
I retreat … in reversal of a magnetic state.
Her potency forces me to float, to glide to gloom,
our once-golden love transmogrified into doom.

# ANTICIPATION

I am looking forward to being
old, when being becomes comic,
not because we grow bandy, or stooped
so a nose must grate against a knee.
Nor is it because the genitalia come
to resemble gherkins and walnuts,
eliciting pity and relief from women,
if not orgiastic hysterical mirth.
Nor does it have a thing to do with the brain.
No, all too cruel, especially for a chap
like me: once so lithe, elastic, quick, erect.
I look forward to being old because
then I can look at myself, and laugh.
Pretension, selfishness, ambition, pride,
achievement, artistry, aplomb, and craft,
inklings of genius, existential pomp,
all collapse into crisp fresh perspective.
Rather than a source of ridicule, I ridicule
myself. I tickle osteoporotic ribs.
I warmly greet the Grim reaper. He slashes
off my head. Reflexly, I catch it, and show
him. He admires a final posthumous grin.

# WANDERER ABOVE A SEA OF FOG

*for Lily*

I am deep below that sea of fog.
I do not comprehend,
and wade through vicious mud,
yearning for Samarkand.

The silence the silence is the worst.
I do not understand.
I'd rather an ear-imploding blast,
some cacophony of great fangs.

It's not quite cold enough for death.
I do not comprehend.
I am kept tepid by thin sheets
and charcoal underpants.

It's not quite warm enough for life.
I do not understand.
The fog feels like pullulating lice,
or featherweight powdery sand.

No, that miasmic foetor is the worst.
I think I understand:
This is a last exhalation of the earth:
our putrefaction: entire, grand.

## CONCLUSIONS

I imagine it's all about unearthing happiness,
the lot that means a lot,
the pilgrimage away from good parents,
and back,
or that unending extrication from the bad.
I imagine it's all about audacity,
not content to be a stick in the sludge,
but conquering a steep escarpment for its vast view,
accosting some rebarbative adversary,
or listening to Aristotle's advice on friends.
I imagine it's all about survival,
the insane search for sanity,
the octogenarian as ox,
a final cackle rather than a choking croak.
I imagine it's all about nothingness,
the vacuum that pursues fulfilment,
the release that is peace,
a terminal diminuendo of the self.

## CLOSURE

I discern the faint footfalls of Doctor Death.
He possesses the daintiest of steps,
as he tippy-toes along my garden path.
A fierce pumpkin moon ignites his skull,
yet his eyes, on pink stalks, display no wrath.
He finds the profession pleasurable,
evaluating death as a form of resurrection.
He desires to add me to his collection.

The Doctor raps knotted knuckles across my
thin door … it opens, silently, on its own.
He hears distant death-rattles, for him a lullaby …
followed by a passacaglia of baritone groans.
Doctor Death floats up flights of stairs,
to find a winding sheet wound around me,
and on my face a concupiscent stare:
the look of a lonely man no longer alone.

## TERRA INCOGNITA

This might have been paradise,
the black, the ochre, and the green,
those vast sootless skies ...
land singing inside a dream ...
days unfurling, furling, in waves,
night a principality of animals.
No kings, captains, slaves,
no prisons, rope, cathedrals,
no guns, bayonets, money,
vice confined to theft of lubras,
infanticide beyond a gunyah,
circumcision out of fear.

We can only imagine, not feel,
our whiteness a blackout there.
The shock enough to make skin peel:
hell, oblivion, despair.

## YEAR ONE

They crucified her,
the mother of Jesus Christ,
on Golgotha,
one year along.
A centurion inserted a spear
up into her birth canal,
and twirled it deftly
between calloused hands.
Another thrust a sponge
dripping with lamb's blood
into her quivering mouth.
Yet another squeezed
Mary's breasts until
they were kneaded bruise-blue.

Nearby, Joseph sawed, and nailed,
constructed his own large cross.

# OLD CEMETERY

*I.M. George Mackay Brown*

Many slabs stand to attention,
those grey and concentrated souls.
Beloved ones are mentioned
in gilt, or by promenading ghouls.

Some lean absurdly to the left,
others topple backwards. Such laughter
tends not to amuse the just bereaved
or those ripe for their hereafter.

Around them the grass knits thick,
mossy, green, made for kneeling knees.
Generous human fertilizer leaks
into subsoils, clay: propitiatory.

We all have a mother a sister buried
inside here, or a father, or a son
buried before his time, one who carried
a sense of duty too far from home.

Yet this seems a place of peace,
where crows caw in E flat major,
where the light slants with warm ease
on marble, granite, our stone tables.

## ODE TO JOY

The end of my day is close.
Dark starlings descend in circles.
The colour of the sunset is rose.
The hours and minutes now hurtle.

I lean on the pine of my verandah,
scrutinize the Evening Star's gleam.
Below, this afternoon's last galah
nibbles away at couch grass seeds.

A cold unseasonal wind erupts
to carpet me in gooseflesh.
Below, Sweetwater Creek flows, perhaps
packed with delicious watercress.

I turn my back on the stars
and their winding sheet: the Milky Way.
I have no appetite. Nausea
has befouled me day after day.

I light a candle by my single bed.
enjoy the old gold of its flame,
watch its guttering until dead,
and know I'm soon to do the same.